Greg Norman

By
Susan Creighton

CRESTWOOD HOUSE
Mankato, Minnesota
U.S.A.

LIBRARY OF CONGRESS CATALOGING IN PUBLICATION DATA

Creighton, Susan.
  Greg Norman
  SUMMARY: A biography of the Australian golfer who began playing when he was sixteen
years old and went on to win many tournaments including the 1986 British Open.
  1. Norman, Greg, 1955-   —Juvenile literature. 2. Golfers—Australia—
Biography—Juvenile literature. 3. British Open Golf Championship—Juvenile
literature. [1. Norman, Greg, 1955-   . 2. Golfers.] I. Title. II. Series.
  GV964.N67C74   1988   796.352'092'4—dc19   [B]   [92]   87-27565
  ISBN 0-89686-371-9

International Standard Book Number:	Library of Congress Catalog Card Number:
0-89686-371-9	87-27565

PHOTO CREDITS

Cover: Focus on Sports
Reuters/Bettmann News Photos: (P. Skingley) 36-37
Focus West: (Fred Vuich) 21; (S. Kendall) 23; (Robert Walker) 35; (Rick Stewart) 41
Journalism Services: 16, 44, 45; (Scott Wanner) 7
Focus on Sports: 4, 10-11, 12, 15, 19, 24, 27, 29, 31, 32, 38-39, 42, 46
UPI/Bettmann News Photos: (Curtis Compton) 47

Produced by Carnival Enterprises.

CRESTWOOD HOUSE

Box 3427, Mankato, MN, U.S.A. 56002

TABLE OF CONTENTS

GROWING UP DOWN UNDER

Celebrating Christmas in the middle of summer might seem odd to most people. But for Greg Norman and his fellow Australians, it is the thing to do. In Australia, summer occurs during our winter, and winter during our summer. That's just the way the seasons work "down under," on the bottom side of the world. And Australia will always be home for Greg Norman.

Gregory John Norman was born on February 10, 1955, in Mount Isa, Queensland, Australia. Greg's father, Merv, was an engineer and executive in a copper mining company. His mother, Toini, was a homemaker who spent much of her time with Greg and his older sister, Janice. While his father was busy managing a company, Greg's mother began introducing him to sports.

As a child, Greg showed a great interest and skill in a variety of sports. Running races, swimming, rugby, squash, Australian-style football, cricket, soccer — he tried them all and was good at most. And growing up in Townsville and Brisbane off the eastern coast of Australia brought Greg into contact with the sea and surf. Even today, waterskiing remains his number-two sport.

"The Great White Shark" impresses fans and fellow golfers with his steady swings.

THE FIRST 18 HOLES

Golf was the one sport that did not seem to be a part of Greg's destiny. Some athletes discover their sport as children, grow with it, and finally become professionals. But Greg didn't even try the game until he was almost 16 years old.

His mother was a good golfer. Toini Norman had a three handicap at the public golf course. Then, as Greg moved into his teenage years, he often caddied for his mother. He pulled Mrs. Norman's golf trolley while she played. But he showed almost no interest in trying the game himself.

"I was enjoying surfing too much," Greg remembers. "I didn't care about golf. I was going to be a pilot in the air force."

One afternoon, Mrs. Norman had finished her game and was having a snack in the clubhouse. Bored, Greg decided to try his hand at golf by playing a couple of holes—and he liked it! The next chance he had, he played his first regulation 18 holes. He shot a score of 108.

Greg had been an enthusiastic athlete for most of his life. But golf became almost an obsession. Here was a game he could really focus his energies on.

Mrs. Norman fed the fires of his enthusiasm. She bought Greg two books to help him develop his game. Both were written by Jack Nicklaus, a famous American golfer. Greg took one book into physics class at Aspley High School and hid it inside his textbook. He studied the book thoroughly and tried out what he learned on the fairways.

Although he had interest in other sports, Greg quickly made golf his number one game.

Greg, who had never liked to study, suddenly had his nose in a book most of the time. Before long, Greg joined the Virginia Golf Club as a junior member with a 27 handicap. Within two years he was playing off scratch (without a handicap). And he was still in school!

Greg can laugh now. "People say I'm a natural golfer. They have no idea of what went into it."

Golf was hard work. Greg's mother would pick him up at school at 3 o'clock to take him to the golf club every day. Greg would practice until dark. Then he would telephone Mrs. Norman, let the phone ring twice and hang up. This was her signal to come and pick him up.

It was 1971. Greg Norman, surfer and waterskier, had found his real calling.

APPRENTICESHIP

Since he was a small boy, Greg had always thought he would be a pilot in the air force. In fact, he had even belonged to the air force cadets, a kind of Australian Boy Scout troop. But now, after graduating from high school, Greg began thinking more seriously about golf. He took a job loading trucks which helped to develop his strength. After work, he continued to hit balls and practice until dark. It was during this time that Greg decided to become a professional golfer.

"I was never particularly good up to that point," Greg says, modestly. "There wasn't much to go on except I had confidence in myself." That confidence would become his gold mine.

Greg moved to Sydney to begin his training to become a pro. There he would get up at 4 a.m. to practice. During the day, he worked in the golf club's shop. In the evening, he would clean up the practice range, picking up thousands of balls. His day was over around 11 p.m.

The work was demanding, but that didn't scare Greg. What really bothered him were the rules the trainees had to follow: three years as an apprentice and no playing in national tournaments. The club seemed to be holding him back.

At last, Greg made a very important decision, one that would shape his future. He moved back to Brisbane and the Royal Greensland Golf Club. A man by the name of Charlie Earp was the pro at Queensland. Charlie took Greg under his wing. Soon, he became the most important figure in Greg's career.

Charlie demanded "length first, accuracy second." He encouraged Greg to take risks, something most golfers are afraid to do. With Charlie's help, Greg developed the long, high drives that are his trademark today.

Charlie also demanded discipline. He insisted that Greg record his practice time and progress every day. He even made a deal with Greg. He let him work half-days in the shop several times a week. In return, Greg had to promise to spend his afternoons "off" practicing. Charlie wasn't kidding. "If I see you going out the club gate at noon, then keep going," he told Greg, "because you're finished!"

Greg watches the ball fly after hitting it with his well-known long, high drive.

In his early training, Greg concentrated on hitting the ball long distances.

Charlie's training paid off. In 1973, just one year after returning to Queensland and meeting Charlie Earp, Greg had won the Queensland Trainees Championship twice. He earned a three-month invitation to play in national tournaments. His first three finishes were fourth, third, and 13th. Then he won the West Lakes Classic by five strokes over David Graham and Graham Marsh. The Classic was only the fourth time Greg had played a 72-hole event!

For a guy who had come late to the game, Greg Norman was quickly learning the ropes. His only teachers had been his mother, Charlie Earp, and a couple of books by Jack Nicklaus.

A PRO—AT LAST!

Under Charlie's watchful eye, Greg was putting his game together. Charlie stressed the long ball off the tee. He thought distance was more important than control early in Greg's training. With his powerful body, Greg was hitting 340-yard drives with ease.

"I would really clobber that ball," Greg said. "I used to hit drives 30 to 40 yards longer than now. But I reduced yardage to gain accuracy."

Greg was beginning to take control of his golf. He had learned to use a valuable tool in his work with Charlie— goal-setting. He used his golf diary to record his goals. He worked on his aim, control, and putting. He experimented with his swing.

At last, in 1976, Greg joined the Australian pro tour. His mother and father were not overjoyed with his choice of careers.

"I hadn't given them a lot of reason to believe I could make it as a professional golfer," he says now. Fortunately, his third time out, Greg won a pro tournament and earned $7,000. His parents breathed a sigh of relief. Maybe there *was* hope that Greg would make it as a pro.

The Australian press began to notice this newcomer with the white-blond hair, blue eyes, and powerhouse drives. Already he was being compared to the great Jack Nicklaus. And before long, Greg would have the chance to meet the man whose books he knew by heart.

1976-1982: THE EARLY YEARS

In 1976, Greg was just 21. It was his first year as a pro. Between that day on the Queensland course with his mother and his first Australian Open, six short years had passed.

The Open was a big event for Greg, and of course he was a little bit nervous. But imagine his surprise at finding out he had been paired with the one-and-only Jack Nicklaus!

Greg was nervous the first day out and finished with an 80 for the round. But the next day, he came in with a respectable 72. Jack told him he thought he was good enough to win in the United States! Greg began thinking about that possibility.

14

The same year, Greg went to Japan and England, and won tournaments there. He went on to play in a number of Asian tournaments, always trying to perfect his game. By the time he was 22, Greg had won tournaments in three different countries. Yet he was still changing his game.

"I was learning," he said. "I was changing my swing. It was too upright. It took me about five years, but I still won at least one tournament every season."

Greg continues to practice and improve his swing.

Between 1977 and 1982, Greg won 11 tournaments in France, Australia, England, Hong Kong, and other countries. By 1982, Greg Norman had become a serious contender in any tournament he chose to enter. Although

he still wasn't winning as consistently as he would have liked, Greg's game kept improving. In 1980, his best season before joining the USPGA tour, Greg earned $240,000. He was making a living at his chosen career, and his reputation was spreading across the globe.

FAMILY LIFE

Any professional athlete can tell a funny story about something unusual that happened on a plane to or from a sporting event. Greg's "airplane story" is about meeting his wife!

In June 1979, Greg was flying home from his first U.S. Open. Laura Andrassy was a flight attendant on that plane. Laura wasn't impressed that Greg was an athlete. She had done charter flights with football and basketball players before. They had behaved rudely, and she had learned to expect that kind of behavior from athletes. But Greg was different. He was polite, a real gentleman.

"He was shy and so was I, but we managed to get a conversation going," Laura says.

Greg insists that Laura started the whole thing. "She sat down next to me," he says.

Whatever *really* happened, Greg and Laura were married in Washington, D.C., on July 1, 1981. They now have two children, a daughter, Morgan-Leigh, born in 1982, and a son, Gregory, born in 1985. They live in the Bay Hill area of Orlando, Florida, not far from Jack Nicklaus and his family.

Greg's daughter gets a golfing lesson from her superstar dad.

THE GREAT WHITE SHARK!

In 1981, Greg received an invitation to play in the U.S. Masters Tournament at Augusta National. He was again paired with his hero Jack Nicklaus. Jack had already won *five* Masters tournaments in his career, not to mention twelve other major tournament victories.

"Take a deep breath and let's enjoy the golf," Jack told Greg. Greg must have been listening, because he played well.

It was after this tournament and all the attention it focused on Greg that he got his nickname.

The reporters had gathered around Greg, following his exciting finish, and were trying to interview him. Someone asked Greg what he liked to do in his spare time. Greg answered that fishing for sharks and hunting were his favorite hobbies. Almost immediately, Greg became known as "The Great White Shark" or simply "Shark." Nicknames, at least in sports circles, do not go away easily. And so, years later, Greg still hears himself called "the Shark." Some fans of his have been known to wear "shark hats" to the tournaments he plays in. And even Morgan-Leigh, his daughter, likes to call him "Sharkey"!

Australian Greg Norman quickly captured the interest of reporters and fans.

GREG'S FIRST PGA TOUR

By 1982, Greg was looking seriously at the U.S. Professional Golf Association (PGA) tour. He had done very well at the 1981 Masters Tournament. He also knew that the real money in golf was on the U.S. tour. And he liked the warm welcome he was receiving from America.

In March of 1983, Greg played his first event as a full-time player on the PGA tour. He lost to golfer Mike Nicolette in a playoff at the Bay Hill Classic. Greg and Mike had been tied at 284 for 72 holes, both 4 under par. It was a good showing for Greg. Although he didn't win a PGA tournament in 1983, he finished 74th overall and qualified for the 1984 tour.

The Australian shark was preparing to take on American golf!

1984: A BIG YEAR

The year started slowly for Greg. By May, he had played in only nine tournaments. He finished in the top 20 only three times. Greg was worried about his game.

He called his old friend, Charlie Earp, back in Australia. Charlie didn't give Greg any technical advice. Instead, he worked on Greg's self-confidence.

"You know you're better than all of those guys!" Charlie told him. "Go out there and beat 'em!"

That must have been just what Greg needed to hear. He

won the Kemper Open in June. Later that same month, he went to the U.S. Open at Winged Foot Golf Club (New York). After making three miraculous pars on the last three holes of the final round, Greg forced a playoff with Fuzzy Zoeller.

In the playoff, Zoeller sank a 68-foot birdie (one stroke under par) putt on the second hole to take a 3-stroke lead.

Greg tackles a tricky shot to get out of a sand trap.

Zoeller was hot. He then ran off eight straight pars and two birdies, to shoot a final 67, the lowest score *ever* in a U.S. Open. Greg double bogeyed (two strokes over par) the second hole and bogeyed (one stroke over par) the third and fourth holes. Even though Greg finished eight strokes behind Zoeller, he was happy to have done so well. Greg walked off the course after the 18th hole smiling, his arm around Zoeller's shoulders.

"In the locker room, Greg had a big smile on his face," said Lawrence Levey, a photographer friend of Greg's. "He said, 'Golf's a funny game, isn't it?' "

Although there were some disappointments, 1984 was a good year for Greg. He finished ninth in the PGA tour standing. Golf-watchers were catching glimpses here and there of the brilliance that Greg's game could deliver. The big question was, could he deliver often enough to become a real heavyweight? Only time would tell!

ILLNESS AND A SLUMP

Greg Norman doesn't have a lucky shirt. He never has. In fact, Greg is not at all superstitious about his game. Other sports personalities may need their good luck coins or special pretournament meals. But Greg has always relied on practice and doing his homework.

"If I'm at home, I will golf between six and eight hours a day—most of that solely on the practice tee. The last ten years I've worked really hard, and the next ten years I'll work even harder. I'll never forget my priorities or where

I want to go."

But 1985 hit Greg like something out of a bad dream. After playing in the Hong Kong Open early in the year, Greg became ill. A persistent hacking cough bothered him both on the golf course and away from it. It was to sap his energy for over a year, casting a dark shadow on his 1985 game.

Before making a putt, Greg takes time out to line up the shot.

"There was something in his chest," said Laura. "We even thought it might be cancer."

Medical tests showed inflamed bronchial tubes in his right lung, along with a mysterious-looking growth.

"I had walking pneumonia," Greg explained. It stayed with him until spring of 1986, when doctors finally diagnosed the illness.

Pneumonia took its toll on Greg and his game. Cyril King, a good friend of Greg's, said, "I've never seen anyone who hates to lose as much as Greg. If you're playing cards with him, or snooker (billiards), or fishing or hunting, he just hates to come in second. This is why he is always going to fulfill the goals he sets himself."

But '85 was not a good year for Greg's goals. He dropped from ninth on the PGA list to 42nd. He won no high honors on the tour.

Even so, Greg never let up during his illness. He worked on his putting, which critics had called the weakest part of his game. He was down, but not out.

As if pneumonia were not enough, an accident almost killed him. In October 1985, Greg was riding a hot dog-shaped tube pulled by a ski boat. Suddenly, Greg fell off into the water and was hit in the face by the foot of another rider. The smash knocked him out. It also knocked out three teeth that ripped his lip apart as well. Greg was lucky to be alive. It took several visits to the hospital and a dentist to patch him up.

Amazing as it seems, just two weeks later Greg led his Australian team to victory in the Dunhill Cup Classic in

Putting has always been a weak spot for Greg and he's worked hard to improve it.

St. Andrew's, Scotland. Pneumonia, dental surgery, and a stitched lip couldn't hold him back!

THE YEAR OF THE SHARK

With antibiotics clearing up his lungs, Greg was back on track in the spring of 1986. This would be a year for the record books!

On April 13, Greg faced his first "major" of the season: the Masters Tournament at Augusta, Georgia. Winning one of the four majors (The U.S. Open, the PGA, the British Open, or the Masters) is the highest honor in golf. Because it's one of the Big Four, the Masters always brings out all the big players. Greg was fired up to play.

The early rounds were encouraging. Greg led at the end of the third round with a 210. Two strokes behind him were Nick Price, Bernhard Langer, Sevi Ballesteros, Tom Watson, Tommy Nakajima, Donnie Hammond, and Tom Kite. Four strokes back, at 214, was his good friend, Jack Nicklaus. The last round was tense, with the lead shifting back and forth among these golfers. Nobody was giving up easily. They all wanted to win.

But, by the 18th tee, Jack and Greg were tied for the lead at nine under par. Jack had no trouble with the hole, parring it and finishing with 65 and a four-round total of 279. Greg needed to par the hole for a tie or birdie for a win. He hit his 3-wood from the 18th nice and straight. But he followed with his 4-iron, which had given him trouble

Looking worried, Greg watches the ball intently.

before. The shot sliced into the gallery. Then his 16-foot putt missed the cup for par. Jack Nicklaus, had surprised everyone by sweeping up his 20th major victory. Greg would have to wait a bit longer for his first.

It was a hard contest to lose. Greg said after the tournament, "I was trying to hit it too hard and too high... I was going for the birdie and the win. It was the first time all week I let my ego get the best of me."

Greg had to settle for a tie for second with Tom Kite.

The next month, Greg won the Panasonic-Las Vegas Invitational. Even though it wasn't a major tournament, it had the biggest prize money on the U.S. tour. Things were looking up!

Then, on June 15th, Greg faced his second major tournament of the year. The U.S. Open would be played at Shinnecock Hills in Southampton, New York.

Again, at the end of the third round, Greg found himself in the lead. Again, he lost the lead in the fourth round. This time, a heckler in the crowd accused Greg of "choking" under the pressure of a near-win. The talk about Greg's fourth-round problems in major tournaments was beginning to follow him, even to the course. Although Greg resumed his play, his final-round 75 was too high for a win. Instead, 43-year-old Ray Floyd captured the U.S. Open. Greg finished in a tie for 12th, six strokes back.

Golf-watchers had begun to look at Greg's performance under pressure. But Greg denied that he had any problems with major tournaments. "I don't let anything bother me, because I know that if I work harder and harder, I'm going to get myself out of it," he said.

At the 1986 U.S. Open, Greg faced another tough loss.

A MONKEY ON HIS BACK?

By the end of June 1986, Greg held the PGA record for highest earnings in a season. His winnings for the year, which was only half over, had already passed a half-million dollars. That was certainly something to smile about!

But more and more, reporters and sports commentators were bringing up a new question. Did Greg have what it took to win a major tournament? Or would he always fall down when the pressure was up?

Greg usually liked talking to sports reporters. He had a reputation for being friendly and open with newspaper and television reporters. But these questions were beginning to upset him.

There is a saying—"He's got a monkey on his back"— which means someone's got an annoying problem he just can't shake. The reporters were saying that Greg had a monkey on *his* back—a monkey that wouldn't let him win a major tournament. To prove them wrong, Greg would have to win a big one.

THE BRITISH OPEN

Greg's next big challenge, the British Open, was held at the Ailsa Course in Turnberry, Scotland, on July 17-20.

The tournament began in a familiar way. By Saturday night, the third round completed, Greg was leading. He was

By the middle of 1986, Greg was playing—and winning—often.

in the winning position for the final round on Sunday. But how many times before had he set himself up in exactly the same way, only to lose it all in the last round? He remembered the bogey on the last hole at the Masters. There was the 75 at Shinnecock Hills that threw the U.S. Open away.

"Everybody knows how much I wanted to win a major," Greg said in Turnberry. "The media is always writing, 'Why can't he win here. Why not there?' and everybody's saying 'Come on, Greggy, do it.' And even if you know you can, it starts to get you down."

At dinner on Saturday night, Jack Nicklaus came over to Greg's table. "Can I talk to you?" he asked. He sat down and told Greg, "Nobody wants you to win this tournament more than I do. You *deserve* to win."

The course was terribly difficult, however. Watered fairways and miserable roughs were only the beginning. The weather was awful. Winds up to 45 miles per hour whipped across the course, and a steady drizzle would not let up.

Lee Trevino, Ray Floyd, Sevi Ballesteros, and Tom Watson all grumbled about the weather. Only Jack Nicklaus remained calm. U.S. golfers are not used to such conditions, and they couldn't overcome them. Fortunately for Greg, he had spent a lot of time on the European circuit in conditions like these.

After the eighth hole at the 1986 British Open, Greg knew he would win the trophy.

Tommy Nakajima of Japan wasn't bothered by the weather either. His father had trained him as a boy to play in wet weather by hitting practice balls under an outdoor shower! He was one shot behind Greg going into the final round.

Nakajima blew the first hole with a double bogey. That gave Greg a three-stroke lead. It became the crucial hole of the day, for Greg would never let his lead drop below three strokes the rest of the afternoon.

At the eighth hole, Greg made a five-foot birdie, stretching his lead to 5. "I think that's when I knew," he said. "When I made that putt, I just said, 'Well, boys, I shut the gate. I'm playing too good now.' "

At the 18th hole, the crowds waited for the new champion. Greg hit the ball to the green and thousands of fans crowded around to watch the putt. In a few moments, it was over. Greg had finished with a 69 for a par 280 over 72 holes — the only golfer to match par in the tournament.

Back in Australia, Greg's parents watched him win on TV. Later that day, Toini Norman went out and won *her* championship! Greg bragged to everyone about his mother's victory!

Greg's prize money of $105,000 would make him the top moneymaker of the year. His second-round 63 tied the British Open record for lowest score ever. But the sweetest thing about the victory was the victory itself. Greg had one his first major!

Greg jokes with other golfers after a tough round at the British Open.

Greg won his first major tournament at the British Open and celebrated the victory with his wife Laura.

FINISHING ON TOP

Greg's next stop on his 1986 U.S. tour was the PGA Championship in Toledo. It was another tense, close contest.

Greg led at the end of three rounds, 202 to Bob Tway's 206. Tway managed to strip away Greg's lead by the 18th hole of the final round to face him dead even. Both men

Although he worked hard at the 1986 PGA Championship, Greg was unable to beat his opponents.

took their opening shots. Then Tway put his second shot in a bunker just short of the green. Greg's second shot landed on the fringe, 25 feet from the cup. Tway swung for his third shot, and the incredible happened. The ball landed on the putting surface and rolled into the cup! He had birdied the hole. Greg needed a miracle, but it didn't come. His ball went past the cup to lose the championship.

It was a tough loss for Greg. But this time, Greg wasn't

shaken. He had proved in the British Open that he was a winner.

He went on to the World Series of Golf at Akron, Ohio, where he tied for 20th place. In September, Greg won the European Open in Sunningdale, England, on the first hole of a playoff against Ken Brown of Britain. Greg won the $52,500 purse (prize money), plus a bonus for becoming the first player to win the British and European Opens in the same year. In September, Greg led the Australian team to a successful defense of its Dunhill Cup title at St. Andrew's, Scotland.

PLANS FOR TOMORROW

When you're 6′1″, 185 lbs., blond, athletic, and handsome, with a beautiful wife and family, a beach home in an exclusive Orlando suburb, you seem to have it all. Add to that a red Ferrari, an Aston Martin, a Rolls Royce, and a Jaguar convertible, there doesn't seem to be much more you could want.

But Greg Norman is just 32 years old as the 1987 season opens. So, of course, he has dreams. "I set daily goals, weekly goals, yearly goals, 20-year goals," he says. "I stimulate myself with goal-setting."

Greg figures he has 15 to 20 major championships ahead of him. With his aggressive game and positive attitude, he's ready for anything. "I don't like to be negative when I

A sand trap shot can't slow Greg down!

Greg tries not to be negative about his game, but enjoys the challenges.

play," Greg says. "I love the challenge. I love grinding. I love it when things aren't going my way and I have to fight for it, fight with myself, and fight for a score. I love having to dig deeper and reach for something."

His loftiest goal is to someday claim the Grand Slam of Golf—the Masters, the U.S. Open, the British Open, and the PGA Championship, all in one year.

It's never been done, but Greg came very close in 1986. He finished first in the British Open and second in the U.S. Open, the Masters, and the PGA Championship. The opening months of 1987 were not as good, but Greg took his losses in stride.

"I've never been in a position where I've lacked the confidence to convert something bad into something good. I've learned so much from all this." You can't help but believe him when he says, "I'll get the Slam one year."

For now, it's more golf, fast cars, fishing, hunting, snooker, and waterskiing. He even likes to take a turn at the controls of a jet airplane. Pilot friends sometimes let him put their planes through a loop or a corkscrew roll. "Anything but take it through the sound barrier!" Greg laughs.

And way down the road? Greg has two flagpoles in front of his house. One carries the U.S. flag, the other the Australian flag. Greg intends to go back home some day.

"I'm hopelessly Australian," he says. "I'd love to be permanently based in Australia, but you can't commute to the British and American tournaments from there. I've

Concentration is tough when playing in front of a crowd.

A moment to relax.

enrolled the kids in a Florida school. I want them to have a stable education, so I'm going to live there for the next 15 years or so. Then I'll go home, buy a cattle station in New South Wales or Queensland, and settle down."

In the meantime, the Great White Shark just keeps on hitting those little white balls!

With his confidence and talent, Greg has what it takes to be a champion.

Greg will continue to improve his game and reach his full potential.

GREG NORMAN'S PROFESSIONAL STATISTICS

Year	Major Tournament Wins	PGA Tour* Position	PGA Money Earned
1979	Hong Kong Open		
1980	French Open, Australian Open		
	Scandinavian Open		
	Suntory World Match Play		
1981	Australian Masters		
	Dunlop Masters		
1982	European Tour Order of Merit		
	Dunlop Masters		
1983	Hong Kong Open	74	$ 71,411
	Kapalua International		
	Suntory World Match Play		
	Australian Masters		
	New South Wales Open		
	Cannes Invitational, Queensland Open		
1984	Kemper Open	9	$310,230
	Canadian Open		
	Australian Masters		
	Victoria Open		
1985	Australian Nissan Cup (team member)	42	$165,458
1986	British Open	1	$653,296
	Panasonic-Las Vegas Invitational		
	Kemper Open		
	Suntory World Match Play		
	Queensland Open		
	Australian Nissan Cup (team member)		
	New South Wales Open		

*Greg Norman joined the PGA Championship Tour in 1983.

48